SESAME STREET

COOKIE MONSTER'S FOODIE TRUCK

A SESAME STREET CELEBRATION OF FOOD

HEATHER E. SCHWARTZ

Lerner Publications ◆ Minneapolis

Lerner Publications Company
An imprint of Lerner Publishing Group, Inc.
241 First Avenue North
Minneapolis, MN 55401 USA

For reading levels and more information, look up this title at www.lernerbooks.com.

Main body text set in Mikado Regular
Typeface provided by HVD Fonts.

Library of Congress Cataloging-in-Publication Data

Names: Schwartz, Heather E., author. | Jim Henson's Sesame Street Muppets, sponsor.
Title: Cookie Monster's foodie truck : a Sesame Street celebration of food / Heather E. Schwartz.
Description: Minneapolis : Lerner Publications, [2020] | Includes bibliographical references and index. | Audience: K to Grade 3. | Audience: Age 6–8 | Summary: "This fun, friendly title based on the Cookie Monster's Foodie Truck segment serves as an introduction to the basics of food literacy"– Provided by publisher.
Identifiers: LCCN 2018043702 (print) | LCCN 2019981045 (ebook) | ISBN 9781541555068 (lb) | ISBN 9781541562196 (ebook)
Subjects: LCSH: Cooking–Juvenile literature. | Cookbooks–Juvenile literature. | Cookie Monster (Fictitious character) | Cooking. sears | Cookie Monster (Fictitious character) sears | LCGFT: Cookbooks.
Classification: LCC TX652.5 .S347 2020 (print) | LCC TX652.5 (ebook) | DDC 641.5–dc23

LC record available at https://lccn.loc.gov/2018043702
LC ebook record available at https://lccn.loc.gov/2019981045

Manufactured in the United States of America
4-50480-42806-3/31/2021

Hello me fellow foodies!

Do you like food like me like food? If answer is yes, this is book for you! Come along on big, fun, food adventure, where lots of surprises await.

Learn about different kinds of healthy foods—like vegetables, fruits, grains, and more. Learn how food grows, and how to measure, mix, and combine lots of yummy ingredients into a dee-licious and healthy recipe for you to eat. *Om nom nom.* Discover which foods are sometimes foods and which are all-the-time foods. (Me like sound of that!)

Wow! All this talking about food making me hungry. Are you hungry? Then place your order with me and friend Gonger. If you lucky, we make you food in our foodie truck!

**From me,
Cookie Monster**

Before we begin, let's wash our hands.

Getting Started

Check the ingredients in each recipe. If you are allergic to something, skip that recipe or have an adult help you find a replacement. People can be allergic to all kinds of things like nuts, dairy, or some kinds of fish.

SOAP

My hands no look dirty.

Germs are invisible! But they can still make you sick. Always wash your hands before cooking and eating.

Me no like germs! Me wash! Me wash!

Be careful while cooking. Always have a grown-up with you. Kids should not touch the oven, knives, food processors, or other sharp objects. Make sure to clean everything when you're finished!

Always Foods and Sometimes Foods

It is important to eat lots of different kinds of healthy foods. You need fruits, vegetables, grains, protein, and dairy. These are "always foods." You can eat them at every meal.

Cookies, ice cream, and other sweets are "sometimes foods." Eat them in small amounts.

Me like the sound of always food. And me *always* like cookies!

No, silly Cookie Monster! Cookies are a sometimes food.

Fruits and Vegetables

Fruits and vegetables are anytime snacks.
They keep your body healthy and strong.

So many snacks, so little time!

Carrots and cucumbers are nice and crunchy. Oranges and berries are sweet and juicy.

There are lots of yummy and healthy snacks to choose from.

Bert and Ernie's Blueberry and Strawberry Salad

Makes 8 servings

Ingredients

2 cups lettuce leaves or other greens

1 cup blueberries

1 cup strawberries

a favorite salad dressing

1. Tear up greens and place in a large bowl.

2. Add blueberries and strawberries.

3. Mix gently.

4. Toss with your favorite dressing.

Blueberries start out small and green. As they grow, they turn pink. Then they turn blue and juicy. They are ripe and ready to pick.

Where we find blueberries?

Look around, Cookie Monster! They grow on bushes.

Blueberries grow on farms or in the wild. Always pick berries with an adult. Some wild berries are not safe to eat!

Tomatoes are my favorite fruit.

What? I thought they were vegetables!

Tomatoes have seeds. That makes tomatoes fruits!

Super Grover's Tomato Soup

Makes 4 servings

Ingredients

3 tablespoons butter

½ large onion

1 can (28 ounces) crushed tomatoes

1½ cups low-sodium chicken broth

salt to taste

1. Have an adult melt butter in a large saucepan.

2. Slice the onion into large wedges. Add to the pan.

3. Add tomatoes, chicken broth, and salt. Stir with a rubber spatula.

4. Simmer uncovered for 40 minutes, stirring occasionally.

5. Cool and blend in a blender.

6. Reheat in the pan and serve.

Tomatoes grow on farms and in gardens. You can also grow a tomato plant in a pot!

Do you know how to find tomatoes, Cookie Monster?

Tomato plants need sunlight and water. New tomatoes start out green. When they turn red, you can pick them and eat them.

That easy. Look for color red!

Eating Your Colors

Red cherries, orange mangoes, and green peas! Make sure to eat foods that are different colors. Each color helps a different part of your body stay healthy and strong.

Make your plate look like a rainbow!

Foods come in many colors. Can you think of a purple food? Do you know of any yellow foods?

Whole Grains

Whole-grain foods are made using all parts of a grain.

Why whole grain called whole grain? Me can eat whole thing?

Yes. But don't eat the plate, Cookie Monster!

Whole-grain foods are full of vitamins and nutrients. They help the body fight disease. They are also tasty! Did you know oatmeal is a whole-grain food? So is brown rice.

This dinner looks positively yucky.

Grundgetta's as-Good-as-Garbage Bowl

Makes 2 servings

Ingredients

½ cup quinoa

1 tablespoon olive oil

1 cup chicken stock

leftovers like vegetables, cooked chicken, beans, chickpeas, or whatever you have!

salad dressing

1. Rinse quinoa in a colander.

2. Ask an adult to heat olive oil in a pan over medium heat. Toast quinoa in oil, stirring constantly for about 5 minutes.

3. Add chicken stock and bring to a boil. Cover and simmer for about 15 minutes.

4. Chop leftovers into bite-sized pieces.

5. Put cooked quinoa in a bowl and add leftovers.

6. Top with your favorite salad dressing.

Only the best for you!

Quinoa is called a whole-grain food because it is prepared and eaten like a grain. But it is really a seed.

Quinoa plants grow in South America where the weather is warm.

In Mexico, we call this *arroz rojo*. It is one of my family's favorite recipes!

Rosita's Red Rice

Makes 6 servings

Ingredients

2 medium tomatoes

1 tablespoon vegetable oil

1 cup long-grain rice

½ small white onion

1 clove garlic, peeled

2 cups chicken broth

½ teaspoon salt

1. Ask for an adult's help with this recipe. First, roast the tomatoes in the oven for 15 minutes at 400°F.

2. Heat the oil in a saucepan. Add rice and cook over medium heat until brown.

3. Blend the roasted tomatoes, onion, and garlic in a food processor.

4. Add the mixture to rice. Heat 3 to 5 minutes, stirring regularly.

5. Add chicken stock and salt. Stir and bring to a boil.

6. Turn down the heat, and simmer until most of the liquid is gone.

7. Turn off the heat. Cover for 5 to 10 minutes.

8. Fluff with a fork and serve. Rosita and her family like to serve this rice with some warmed-up red beans!

Rice grows in wet fields in Asia. A rice field is called a rice paddy. Farmers drain the water out of the paddy. Then they cut the plants.

A couple of days later, they separate the rice from the plant.

Dairy and Protein

Do you want strong bones and healthy teeth? Eat dairy! Butter, milk, cheese, and yogurt are dairy foods.

Dairy mean milk, right? Time for milk and cookies!

Protein can also help you grow strong. Seafood, chicken, eggs, and beans are filled with protein.

Some foods such as yogurt, milk, and cheese have both dairy *and* protein!

Try some yogurt, Cookie! That's dairy too. And it's also a good source of protein.

Peanut Butter and Fruit Smoothie

Makes 1 serving

Ingredients

½ cup milk of your choice

2 tablespoons creamy peanut butter

½ cup sliced strawberries

½ cup ice cubes

~~~~~~~~~~~~~

1. Add all ingredients into a blender.

2. Blend until smooth.

3. Pour into a glass and serve.

This tastes good.

It's nice and cold. And it's fun to slurp up with a straw!

Where does milk come from? After a cow has a calf, her body makes milk for the next eleven months or so. That's a lot of milk!

Cows are milked two or three times a day. Then the milk is packaged and brought to stores for people to buy.

> Is chicken an always food or a sometimes food, Gonger?

Sesame Street Chicken
Makes 4 servings

Ingredients
1 cup flour

1 teaspoon salt

½ teaspoon black pepper

4 boneless, skinless chicken breast halves, sliced into strips

¼ cup plus ½ teaspoon sesame oil

¼ cup low-sodium soy sauce

¼ cup brown sugar

2 tablespoons sesame seeds, toasted

1 tablespoon chopped chives

1. Combine flour, salt, and pepper in a gallon-size plastic bag. Shake to mix.

2. Add chicken strips a few at a time. Seal bag and shake to coat the chicken.

3. Ask an adult to heat ¼ cup sesame oil in a skillet.

4. Add chicken strips. Cook over medium heat for about 4 minutes until they are not pink inside.

It's an always food, Elmo. It has lots of good protein.

5. Remove chicken and set it aside on a plate.

6. Add soy sauce and sugar to the skillet. Cook until sugar dissolves, stirring occasionally.

7. Add ½ teaspoon oil and sesame seeds to the skillet.

8. Toss the chicken in the sauce and warm to reheat. Sprinkle with chopped chives for garnish and serve.

Sesame plants grow in warm parts of Asia and East Africa. The seeds are shaken off a dried plant.

But they're not ready to eat yet. First, they are taken out of their dark shells. Some sesame seeds are white. Others are black, red, brown, or tan.

Setting the Table

Before it's time to eat, set the table. The napkin and fork go on the left of the plate. The spoon and knife go on the right. Count one plate, one napkin, and one set of silverware for each person coming to dinner.

How many people are coming to dinner?

Let's count. Cookie Monster, Zoe, and Abby are coming to dinner. And so are you, Elmo! That's one, two, three, four!

Time to Eat!

The best part about cooking is sharing the meal with your family and friends!

Glossary

allergic: to be sick after eating, touching, or breathing something

broth: a liquid in which meat or vegetables have been cooked

harvest: to gather crops from a field

ingredient: one of the items used to make a food dish

nutrient: a substance people, plants, and animals need to live and grow

ripe: ready to be picked or eaten

silverware: tools for eating such as a fork, knife, or spoon

simmer: to cook something at a low heat until it is almost boiling

vitamin: a natural substance found in foods that helps keep your body healthy

Further Information

Butterworth, Chris. *How Did That Get in My Lunchbox? The Story of Food.* Somerville, MA: Candlewick, 2011.

Choose My Plate
https://www.choosemyplate.gov/kids

DK. *Are You What You Eat?* New York: DK, 2015.

Kid's Healthy Eating Plate
https://www.hsph.harvard.edu/nutritionsource/kids-healthy-eating-plate/

Sesame Street
https://www.sesamestreet.org/

Waldendorf, Kurt. *Hooray for Chefs.* Minneapolis: Lerner Publications, 2017.

Index

Photo Acknowledgments

Image credits: Zurijeta/Shutterstock.com, p. 7; samael334/iStockphoto/Getty Images, p. 8; iMoved Studio/Shutterstock.com, p. 8 (inset); Valentina Razumova/Shutterstock.com, p. 10 (berries); Preto Perola/Shutterstock.com, p. 10 (apple); Volosina/Shutterstock.com, p. 10 (carrots); spaxiax/Shutterstock.com, p. 11 (cucumber); topseller/Shutterstock.com, p. 11 (orange); LanaSweet/Shutterstock.com, p. 12 (background); Kati Finell/Shutterstock.com, p. 13; Trong Nguyen/Alamy Stock Photo, p. 14 (background); Trong Nguyen/Shutterstock.com, p. 15; Boltenkoff/Shutterstock.com, p. 16 (tomato); M Kunz/Shutterstock.com, p. 16 (tomato); djedzura/Getty Images, pp. 17, 45 (soup); Richard Felber/Getty Images, pp. 18-19 (background); Viktar Malyshchyts/Shutterstock.com, p. 20 (fruit); bergamont/Shutterstock.com, p. 21 (bananas); Pektoral/Shutterstock.com, p. 21 (eggplant); zarzamora/Shutterstock.com, p. 21 (bowl); maxbelchenko/Shutterstock.com, pp. 22-23 (background); VasiliyBudarin/Shutterstock.com, p. 23 (oatmeal); MSPhotographic/Shutterstock.com, pp. 23, 44 (rice); Westend61/Getty Images, pp. 25, 45 (garbage bowl); Jay S Simon/Getty Images, pp. 26- 27; everydayplus/Shutterstock.com, p. 27 (Quinoa); M Kunz/Shutterstock.com, p. 28; Lapina Maria/Shutterstock.com, p. 29; Marko Konig/imageBROKER RF/Getty Images, pp. 30-31 (background); Thorsten Milse/Robert Harding World Imagery/Getty Images, p. 31; Daniel Hurst Photography/Moment/Getty Images, p. 32 (background); Bruno Crescia/Design Pics/Getty Images, p. 33 (beans); Veaceslav Cernat/EyeEm/Getty Images, p. 33 (eggs); manaemedia/Shutterstock.com, p. 33 (strawberries); OlegSam/Shutterstock.com, p. 33 (cheese);Janine Lamontagne/Getty Images, pp. 34, 45 (smoothie); Valentyn Volkov/Shutterstock.com, p. 35 (strawberries); Chee Siong Teh/EyeEm/Getty Images, p. 35 (peanut butter); Christy Strever/EyeEm/agency/Getty Images, p. 36 (cows); Steve Baccon/Getty Images, p. 37; October22/Shutterstock.com, pp. 39, 44 (chicken); Grant Dixon/Getty Images, pp. 40 -41 background); kiboka/Shutterstock.com, p. 41 (inset); Todd Strand/Independent Picture Service, p. 42 (background); S_Photo/Shutterstock.com, pp. 44-55 (table); Elena Veselova/Shutterstock.com, p. 45 (green bowl).

Cover: Maks Narodenko/Shutterstock.com; Food1.it/Shutterstock.com; Valentina Razumova/Shutterstock.com; M88/Shutterstock.com; virtu studio/Shutterstock.com.